WHAT
NOT
TO NAME
THE BABY

By Roger Price and
Leonard Stern

WITH COUNTLESS ILLUSTRATIONS BY PETER MARKS
SUITABLE FOR FRAMING, SENDING TO FRIENDS
OR STICKING PINS IN.

PRICE / STERN / SLOAN
Publishers, Inc., Los Angeles

TWELFTH PRINTING – JANUARY, 1974

COPYRIGHT © 1960, THE PRICE-STERN CORPORATION
ALL RIGHTS RESERVED. THIS BOOK, OR PARTS THEREOF,
MAY NOT BE REPRODUCED IN ANY FORM WITHOUT PERMISSION.

PARTS OF THIS BOOK ORIGINALLY APPEARED IN *PLAYBOY*,
A SPLENDID MAGAZINE THAT WE ALL SHOULD READ.
LIBRARY OF CONGRESS CATALOG NO.: 60-12559

ISBN: 0-8431-0047-8

*"A good name
is rather to be chosen than
great riches"*
                    Proverbs 22:1

FOREWORD

Sticks and stones will break my bones,
But names will never hurt me!

DUE TO THE UNFORTUNATE *and widespread acceptance of the above couplet as truth, the great fields of Name Research and Name Analysis have been overlooked for centuries. In an effort to solve the riddle of human personality, scholars have foolishly gone off into the blind alleys of Psychoanalysis, Biochemistry, Graphology, Economic Determinism, Genetics and Numerology and have ignored the basic fact that—*

A rose by any other name could be a gardenia.

The little verse concerning sticks and stones is a categoric nontruth. Sticks and stones, of course, can hurt you—although the possibility in this age of the switchblade knife and the three-hundred-horse-power auto-

mobile is slight—but the damage they do can usually be repaired. However, the harm derived from a bad or a wrong Name is permanent. In fact:

> Sticks and stones will break your bones,
> But names can really louse you up good.

Savages have always realized the importance of Names and even today certain primitive societies such as the Kikuyus, the Zulus and Members of Athletic Clubs * try to keep their True Names a secret, feeling that if their enemies discover them they will be able to work all sorts of unpleasant sympathetic magic upon them.

American Indians had a more positive approach and seriously attempted to give their offspring names that would guarantee them strength and virtue. Names such as RUNNING DEER (*a name which would tend to influence the child to become graceful and speedy*), TALL MAN WHO HUNTS AT NIGHT, GRAY BADGER WITH MANY SCALPS *or* BUFFALO HUNTER.

Now if we wanted to make sure that our children were successful according to the more elaborate standards of the white man's culture, we could give them up-dated versions of these Names. For instance we might call a son, APPLE POLISHER WHO ALWAYS GETS A RAISE, *or* OWNS MANY HOUSES, GETS AROUND RENT CONTROLS *or* COOL CAT WHO MAKES OUT PLENTY *or* perhaps simply, TAX EVADER.

And we could give girls helpful names such as WALKS WITH WIGGLE, *or* GOES TO COLLEGE, MARRIES DOCTOR, *or* LITTLE MINK WITH MOVIE CONTRACT, *or* SMOOTH CHICK WHO GET MUCH ALIMONY.

* This is not meant to be facetious. You should hear some of the unlikely nicknames the aging handball players call each other.

On examination we can see, of course, that names such as these would obviously be impractical; so in naming your children you will have to be content with the regular name-type Names, which in their own subtle way can have as strong an influence upon a child's personality as the more direct Indian Names.

The rest of this book will, if you approach it with an open mind, a pure heart and a dry Martini, enable you to understand the hitherto mysterious and connotative effects of Names and to start your child off in any direction you choose merely by naming it correctly.

Fair enough?

WHAT
NOT
TO NAME
THE BABY

*The Price-Stern theory of Names explained
for the first time in any language*

WHEN I WAS GOING to grade school back in Charleston, W.Va., we never heard of Dr. Freud or words like "hostile" or "insecure." We were, nevertheless, aware of different personality types among us, and we could define them merely by saying: "So-and-so is a Jerk," or "So-and-so is Swell," or "So-and-so is a Keen First Baseman."

Later I began to think seriously about the peculiar differences between people. It was right after a girl named CARLOTTA, the local optician's daughter, had shown a singularly clear-cut preference for a tall, curley haired athlete named LANCE. I couldn't understand why she preferred him to me. I made better grades than he did and could help her with her geometry. And her mother liked me the best. I finally decided it was all because of our Names. He looked and acted like LANCE, and I was a pure, 100 per cent ROGER.

Inasmuch as similar situations came up repeatedly as I grew older, I spent a great deal of time thinking about this phenomenon and recently began discussing it with my friend, Leonard Stern. Eventually we worked out a whole theory about personality based on the idea that people generally become the kind of person their Name sounds like they should be. Our theory not only makes as much sense as any other theory about personality, but it's also more fun and easier to explain than any of the others. I'll explain it.*

All babies, when they are first born, are just about the same. Until a baby is given a Name it has no personality and to the casual observer, not even any sex. It is nothing but a dampish, noisy lump. But once you give the baby a Name society begins to treat it as if it had the type of personality the name implies, and the child, being sensitive, responds consciously and unconsciously and grows up to fit the name.

Take myself.

* While working out the theory Mr. Stern had most of the ideas which is why I got stuck with the typing.

According to available evidence I was once a dampish, noisy lump myself, with no opinions, no attitudes and no collection of neckties. If I had never been given a Name, I might have grown up to become merely a larger, noisier lump. To be less hypothetical, if my parents and friends, during my formative years (from 1 to 35) had referred to me only as "Hey, you!" it's logical to assume that I wouldn't be overly self-confident or get invited to many parties. (Actually, I don't get invited to many parties as is; but Mr. Stern assures me it's not because I have no personality, it's because I have too much.) But fortunately my parents decided to give me a Name, and they picked out ROGER.

Now in the nineteen twenties the name ROGER was identified almost exclusively with stuffy little boys in comic strips and Our Gang comedies who wore thick eyeglasses, were teacher's pets and who made the best grades in school. I don't know *how* this affected me, but I do know that at the age of nine I was wearing eyeglasses, and possibly because the other kids used to tease me about it (Hey, Four Eyes!) I accepted the fact that I looked studious and eventually made the best grades in school and gave the class oration at commencement.

However, according to the Price-Stern theory, if I had been named NICK, I'm sure my eyes would have been as sharp as an eagle's. I would have developed an early interest in card games, and instead of studying, I would have been playing hookey, shooting marbles for keeps, and organizing games of pitch penny in the school basement. By now I would be a pit boss in Las Vegas.

If, on the other hand, my mother and father had hit upon the name LEO, I would have gained eight pounds within the week. At seventeen I would have been an All-State Fullback and today, after playing pro-football for six years I would have had a broken nose, a trick knee and a job selling sporting equipment.

And what would have happened if they had named me DWIGHT? Who can tell?

Just think for a moment about the people you know. Are you thinking? Good. Don't most of their names fit them? Or according to the P–S theory, don't most of them fit their names? Can you imagine that gangly blond fellow from Wisconsin who works in the market being called PORFIRIO? If this fellow (whose name is WALTER, CARL or RALPH) had been named PORFIRIO, he would have stopped growing four inches sooner and would have shiny black hair. He would never have owned a pair of blue jeans. He would have developed an early talent for doing the cha-cha and for kissing girls on the shoulder, and he would have had to leave town before he graduated from high school.

To show the scientific basis for this reasoning let me cite two imaginary—and far fetched—examples: Suppose we have a boy lump, or technically, a baby, who is mistakenly called LUCILLE. Take my word for it. Stranger things have happened. Now everyone calls this baby LUCILLE and it grows up responding to society's idea of what LUCILLE should be like. In one way or another, this baby, at the age of eighteen, is going to have a problem. Especially when it tries to get off-the-shoulder party dresses to fit properly.

Or suppose a baby were called GOOF-BALL. It's parents, teachers and friends all called it GOOF-BALL. As it grew older, the child would get the idea that people seemed to think of him as being something less than a genius, and, by the time he was twenty, he would still be having trouble with the multiplication table and would consider it an accomplishment when he managed to tie his shoelaces.

To be more realistic, there was a boy in my class back home whose parents named him HERSCHELL—which you must admit is a pretty dopey name. And HERSCHELL was a pretty dopey kid. When you were in school wasn't there at least one dopey kid? And didn't he have a dopey name? Working backwards, the chances of a dopey kid having dopey parents are better than average and parents who would name their son HERSCHELL probably weren't exactly world-beaters? *

Actually, if HERSCHELL *hadn't* been a dopey kid we would have automatically given him a nickname, such as WHITEY, or BUCK or MOOSE, that would have suited him. But we didn't. He was a genuine HERSCHELL.

Girls even more than boys seem to fit their names. Think of the MARYS you know. Aren't they even-tempered, sweet and demure? SUSANS are energetic and cute and bake cookies. RITAS are troublemakers. CLARES tend

---

* If your name is HERSCHELL and you were a dopey kid you may have your money back on this book if you send us a notarized statement to this effect.

to wear tight clothes and insist that men light their cigarettes. LILLIANS tell their troubles to everyone. However, if they are called LIL, everyone tells their troubles to them.

JOANS wear powder blue and pearls and are the ones fellows want to marry. FLORA has a large bust and is embarrassed by it and wears dickeys.

MADELINES become executives in Women's Clubs and organize charity drives. LOUISE and HELEN do all the work, but MADELINE gets all the credit. She owns fourteen pairs of white gloves.

CLARA has good posture and a severe hairdo. CLARAS make excellent husbands for indecisive men and raise their children scientifically.

Give a girl a name like JANE and in no time she will be a little too heavy around the hips and will wear the same hairdo she did in high school. She will be friendly, rather than flirty, because people expect JANES to be that way. If this same girl had been named CHLOE (or CARLOTTA), however, she would feel a compulsion to wear blue eye shadow, would develop an undulating walk and would wear daisies at her waist.

CAROLS are big boned, healthy girls who get married young and have three children.

ARLENES have big eyes and talk a lot. CHARLOTTES like to be a Pal to their men friends and wear heavy black glasses.

GERTRUDES, when young, tend to have too many teeth and dull hair; but they improve themselves. By the time they're seventeen, they're called either TRUDY or GERT depending on whether they become cute or smart.

WHAT NOT TO

AGATHAS wear pink, transparent nylon blouses and babushkas and are either overweight or underweight.

JACKIES are small, sparkly, and neat. They wear ribbons in their hair and full skirts with crinoline petticoats and like to dance with tall men.

MARILYNS are always on a diet and make excellent secretaries.

CHRISTINE was the first girl in her class to peroxide her hair.

NORMA and IRMA are tall and broad shouldered and wear tailored suits. NORMA slouches, but IRMA doesn't. They're both good sports.

JUDY has a pony tail and never gets over being cheer leader in high school. She marries a fellow who thinks she's the greatest.

EILEEN is a flirt and drinks Alexanders and Daiquiris. After the fourth one she can be coaxed into anything.

PEGGY likes physical contact. PEGGY is always punching you in the ribs, and she likes to Indian wrestle and see who has the strongest grip. No matter how hard you squeeze, PEGGY never winces.

YVONNE becomes a co-respondent.

A girl called LAURA will be delicate, or at least look delicate. There are a lot of things LAURA can't eat and no one is quite sure how long she's going to be around She lives to be ninety-two.

VIOLA goes around telling everyone she just lost twenty-two pounds; but no one can tell the difference. IRIS has freckles and marries a Professional Man.

GEORGIA is the one at the party who makes the other

girls mad by kissing all the husbands and dancing the rhumba "the way they do in Cuba."

CONNIE always takes up with men who treat her badly.

Girls whose names have tricky spelling—JAYNE, TERI, MILI, MARSHA, MARYANE, BETTE, etc.—are special cases. The names look theatrical and these girls tend to gravitate toward the more flamboyant professions such as acting, modeling and painting. They are sometimes successful. They come in assorted shapes and sizes.

But to get back to men:

TOM, of course, is the solid citizen of the world. He's dependable and makes a fine husband whose only fault is a tendency toward hyperacidity as he gets older. TOM is a Good Guy.

TOMMY, however, is an entirely different fellow. TOMMY figures the world owes him a living and he is clever enough to collect it. TOMMY lets his hair fall over his forehead, wears sports jackets, borrows money, and plays tennis. His attitude toward females is predatory. He brings them little presents and eventually marries an older woman who has a little something put aside.

TONY is the same as TOMMY.

ANTHONY is nothing like TONY. ANTHONY has large, beautiful eyes and used to be an altar boy. He always hangs a flag outside his house on Columbus Day.

JIMS AND JIMMYS are the ones girls want to marry.

Then there's GEORGE. If you name your son GEORGE, as soon as he gets old enough people start imposing on him. He is good-natured. He puts on a little weight, and, when he's thirty-two, marries the plain sister of a

17

WHAT NOT TO

friend more or less as a favor. Later he loses a lot of money on a tip his wife's father gives him on the stock market.

But if the same baby is called JOE he becomes a JOE. He thinks before he says anything and speaks slowly. By the time he's twelve he knows how to fix broken toys for the younger kids. When he grows up he never does too well in business because he's always cosigning a bum loan or extending too much credit. He seldom leaves the town he was born in.

Although he can be counted on for small loans JACK isn't anything like good old GEORGE or TOM. Everyone likes JACK but no one loves him. JACK is essentially lonely. He pals around with STANLEY.

LOU is someone's husband. He has a big stomach and chews on cigars. LOU overtips in restaurants.

OSCARS are C.P.A.'s who wish they were doctors and who drop names.

EARL is a small fellow with no chin and a deep voice who marries a big woman. MARK and WOODROW are popular teachers in a Midwestern college.

HARRY always knows where to get some more ice.

If you call your child ALBERT or ALFRED, chances are he'll become a scientist or get some kind of a job that requires using his brains. However, if you start calling him AL, he will grow up to be a salesman. AL is always selling something, even if its only himself. AL knows all the angles and can fix a traffic ticket or get you a seat on an airplane or a rate at a resort hotel.

ALAN is someone else entirely. He is a well-mannered, nice-looking boy with a rosy complexion who's always sort of a disappointment to the girls who were anxious to date him. ALAN may get married but at the age of forty-two he is a plumpish bachelor who cooks.

ALVIN has fat, hairy legs and wears garters.

MARTY and BERNIE hang around ranches and ski resorts but they don't ride or ski. They drink Manhattans and wear the clothes.

PETER does ride and ski and is an amateur artist. He wears a Tattersall vest.

PETE wears the vest that came with the suit and is heavier than PETER. PETE smokes cigars and belongs to a bowling team. The other members of the team are FRED, HANK, and GUS. These fellows are married to ETHEL, MARION, FLORENCE, and MILLY, who have a bridge club. MILLY plays the silliest, but she always wins.

Being an unusually intelligent person—after all you purchased this book—you have no doubt realized by this time that the Theory of Names is not based upon the Name that people use to sign their checks or that is on their birth certificate. It is based on the Name that friends and relatives, with the possible exception of their Mother, called them from the time they were nine or ten until they graduated from High School.

Most people, we believe, are called mostly by one Name. For instance, a PATRICIA who is over average in height, has good posture and is dark is called "PAT." Whereas if she happens to be blond and bouncy she is "PATSY" or "PATTY." I have a friend named WALT who is a pure WALT. No one ever calls him WALTER or WALLY, who are two other people.

You will find, I believe, that the vast majority of us have one basic Name. Sometimes people who don't know us very well—usually AL or HOWIE—will call us by an inappropriate diminutive. They'll call WALTER "WALLY" or call LEO "LEE" or call me "ROG." (No one, except AL and HOWIE, has ever called me anything but "ROGER.")

Naturally, along with other people in the scientific-theory game (Freud, William James, Einstein, Galileo, etc., etc.), Mr. Stern and I realize and accept the possibility of error in our findings. Occasionally you will find flagrant exceptions to the conclusions expressed here. These exceptions merely prove the validity of our Theory.

But before saying you know a CONNIE who is a Man-Killer or a PETER who is a slob, stop and think if perhaps there aren't extenuating circumstances that makes these *special cases* rather than *exceptions*. Perhaps this CONNIE *was* treated badly by a man, or men, and is getting her revenge. Maybe that PETER was raised within an ethnic or racial group where the connotations we speak of are different. No attempt has been made to analyze the effect of specific cultural or provincial names on children. MING TOY for example is probably quite distinct from C'HIN TSO-LIN; but we don't profess to know how or why. Other studies could be made of names used in special sections, such as the Deep South. As soon as the Ford Foundation comes through with a grant, we will get with it.

Legitimate exceptions to the Price-Stern theory of Names include most actors and people in public professions, who often have manufactured names and public personalities.

Then there are other names which are so widely held that they are neutral and exert little influence upon a child: WILLIAM, JOHN, ROBERT, MARGARET, CATHERINE,

ANN, and ELIZABETH. But, as a child with one of these standard names grows up, he often gets a nickname—many of which have been noted here—which will fit his personality. Or vice versa.

Here are some more Male Names in a sort of alphabetical order:

ADOLPH
See page 125

ALEXANDER is a con man.

ALAN
See page 18

ALEX is a hard worker who never bothers anyone. He always gets invited to the parties, but no one notices if he doesn't come.

ALVIN
See page 19

ALBERT, ALFRED or **AL**
See page 18

ANDREW—When ANDREW has a date, he makes suggestive remarks and tries to proposition her right away. When the girl turns him down, he feels he's done his duty, so he can relax and be pleasant. Once, a girl took him up on it, and he started sneezing and broke out in spots.

WHAT NOT TO

ANDY worked his way through school. If you're in trouble, ANDY is a good fellow to ask for help.

ANTHONY
See page 17

ARNOLD acts superior when you light a cigarette. He tells you how long its been since he stopped smoking. He feels great; his appetite is better, and he doesn't cough in the morning.

ARTHUR is forty-six years old and is planning to get married as soon as he's ready to settle down. He buys the New York *Times*, but never reads it.

ART works for a big company and dresses neat; but he's secretly a Beatnik.

ARTIE'S shoes are always shined. He is something like AL only not as successful. ARTIE can get you hi-fi parts, electric blenders, and cheap watches at a discount—not wholesale, but at a discount. This way, ARTIE makes a little profit.

AUGUST comes between July and September.

AUGIE used to be a guard on the football team and is always breaking things or stepping on the cat. AUGIE likes DORIS, but once she saw him wipe his nose on his sleeve and won't have anything to do with him.

AUSTIN is the fellow who takes your car when you park it in a lot. The guys he works with call him a name based on the state he came from like TEX (Or MISSISSIP). He has short blond hair, and, when he takes off in your car, he guns the motor and spins the wheels and you have the feeling he's not going to stop until he gets to Fort Worth. When there's a dent in your fender, the boss says "TEX musta did that," but TEX is gone now. The fellow who takes his place is called ARKY.

BARNEY is a hard-working slob who tucks his napkin into his collar and drinks beer with his meals. He works like a dog to send his kids through an Ivy League college, and after they graduate he can't understand why they don't seem to approve of him.

BARRY asks girls to pick him up at his apartment. When they get there, BARRY is in a bathrobe and says, "I got hung up on the telephone, Honey. Still haven't had time to take a shower. You make yourself at home." Then when he gets in the shower he keeps hollering out, "Hey, how'd you like to wash my back?" This makes the girls sore and they leave. The only one who doesn't leave is VIRGINIA. (*See page 27.*)

BERT wishes he were athletic and is always trying to get up a Ping-pong game. He hangs around with GORDIE.

BORDEN sniffles.

BILL, nothing much could be wrong with anyone called BILL.

NAME THE BABY

BARRY

WHAT NOT TO

BERNARD never seems to have much fun.
(*See page 29.*)

BERNIE
See page 19

BOBBY—Never lend money to Bobby.

BRAD invites you to someone's house. When you get there, they don't seem too happy to see either one of you.

BROOKE is charcoal gray.

BROTHER—Anyone, over the age of eight, who is called Brother, Sonny or Buddy takes pills.

BOMBO likes bananas. If he isn't a chimpanzee, he's in trouble.

BRICK played drums one summer with a local band, so he thinks of himself as a musician. He accompanies juke boxes by playing imaginary piano on the edge of the table.

NAME THE BABY

BERNARD

WHAT NOT TO

BRUCE—When your sister brings a girl friend home from school, you get the friend a date with BRUCE. He looks okay and won't make trouble. (*See page 31.*)

BOB (see BILL).

CARL sweats a lot.

CHARLES likes to hang around with his father's friends. He uses dental floss.

CHARLEY gives you a good horse in the sixth race.

CHESTER is very active in Alchoholics Anonymous.

C'HIN TSO-LIN
See page 20

CHRISTOPHER looks good in tweeds and seems to be a natural leader. He's actually the most henpecked guy in the neighborhood.

NAME THE BABY

BRUCE

WHAT NOT TO

CHRIS has stereophonic sound, wears a cap, and likes to make salads.

CHUCK has a crew cut and wears a T-shirt with a jacket over it with only the bottom button buttoned. CHUCK still talks about the time Johnny Lujack was quarterback for the Chicago Bears.

CLARENCE still wears double-breasted suits. When CLARENCE goes to a restaurant, he always orders the same thing.

CLARK
See page 125

CLAY is the big blond guy at the beach who kicks sand on ninety-seven-pound weaklings.

CLIFF goes to the barber shop twice a week and talks loud. He likes to tell you how much everything he owns cost.

CURT (**or KURT**) has only been in the country a year. He says "Ja" instead of "Yes" and keeps telling you he's Swiss even though you haven't asked him. Curt always tries to make out with your girl, asks for her phone number right in front of you—makes you feel like two cents. (See page 34.)

DANNY has a wife who's smarter than he is.

DAVID—When you meet DAVID you think he's a snob, but everyone says he is really just shy. They're wrong. He is a snob.

DAVE puts on weight. He's jolly around the boss or customers, but is miserable to waitresses and people who work for him.

DENNIS always has to leave early to drive his mother someplace.

DEWEY looks like AUSTIN only he has a bigger adam's apple. DEWEY is the night cook in a diner and when you go in he's

WHAT NOT TO

CURT (or KURT)

NAME THE BABY

always talking to the waitress who's just leaving. Her name is FRAN, and no matter when you get there she's just getting dressed in a little back room full of Coke-bottle cases. You can almost see into the room, but not enough. She comes out and stands in the door with her coat on and talks to DEWEY while she's waiting for a red-headed guy in a jalopy to pick her up. DEWEY never looks at her while he's talking. He keeps scraping the hot plate. DEWEY likes to make milk shakes, and when he opens the icebox to get the milk you can see one steak in there, a real steak, not a minute steak. You figure DEWEY is saving that one for himself. He waits till the right time to fix it. DEWEY doesn't ring everything up on the cash register, and the next time you go in they've fired him; the new cook is an older, thinner fellow named LES. Sometimes, you wonder if DEWEY ever sees FRAN anymore.

DINO
See page 125

DICK is neat and in school he was voted the Most Likely to Succeed. He almost did.

WHAT NOT TO

DONALD was once a Four-H-Club Winner. He walks like he's not quite used to pavement.

DON is a friend of HOWARD's. DON pats his wife on the back when he gets home instead of kissing her. He has a power lawn mower.

DOUGLAS smokes a pipe and does exercises with bar bells. He marries JUDITH. They were high-school sweethearts, but JUDITH wanted to "be sure," so they decided she would go to the City for a year. By the end of the year she realized she couldn't do any better, so he came and got her.

DUKE has straight black hair and wears a leather jacket and jeans. DUKE always looks like he crashed the party, even when the party is at his house. (*See page 37.*)

NAME THE BABY

DUKE
and FLEUR

DOUG is a Madison-Avenue type. He was big in School Politics and likes to hold the telephone with his shoulder and sign letters while he's talking to someone.

DWIGHT
See page 13

ED is active in a veteran's organization and is always telling you what he read in the *Reader's Digest*. Don't argue with ED. It's a waste of time. (*See page 39.*)

EARL
See page 18

EDDIE is an assistant. He buys girly picture books.

ELLIOTT wishes he could get a job in London. He quotes Winston Churchill and wears suspenders, but calls them "braces," and gets very peeved if you write his name, leaving off the last T.

ELMER—No one is ever *really* called ELMER.

EMMET belongs to a chess club and knows the names of all the openings and gambits;

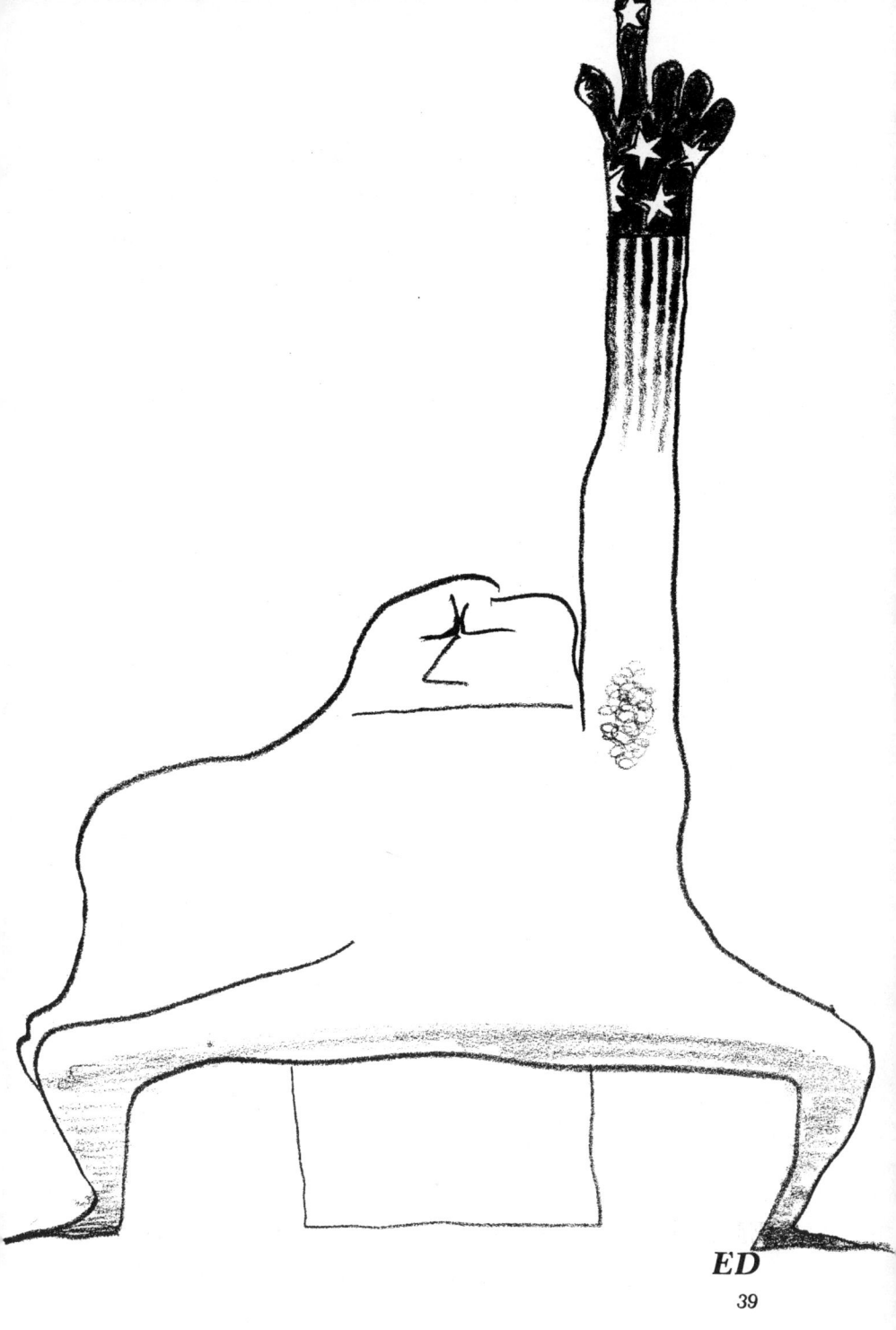

yet, if you play chess with him, he never wins. However, he isn't upset, and he will explain at length why you beat him. He also explains to girls why they don't love him. In school, he explained to the coach why he couldn't make the team. In time, he may explain to the Doctor why he can't be cured.

ERIC wears expensive shirts and combs his hair a lot. He comes to parties without a date and confuses the girls by flirting with all of them. (*See page 41.*)

ERNIE was an officer during the war and hasn't been the same since he got out of the service. He has a collection of insignia and will show you color slides he took overseas. On Saturdays, ERNIE wears his officer's-shirt, the one with shoulder straps on it.

EVERETT is homely.

FRANCIS is handsome and fun; but his friends wish he wouldn't drink so much.

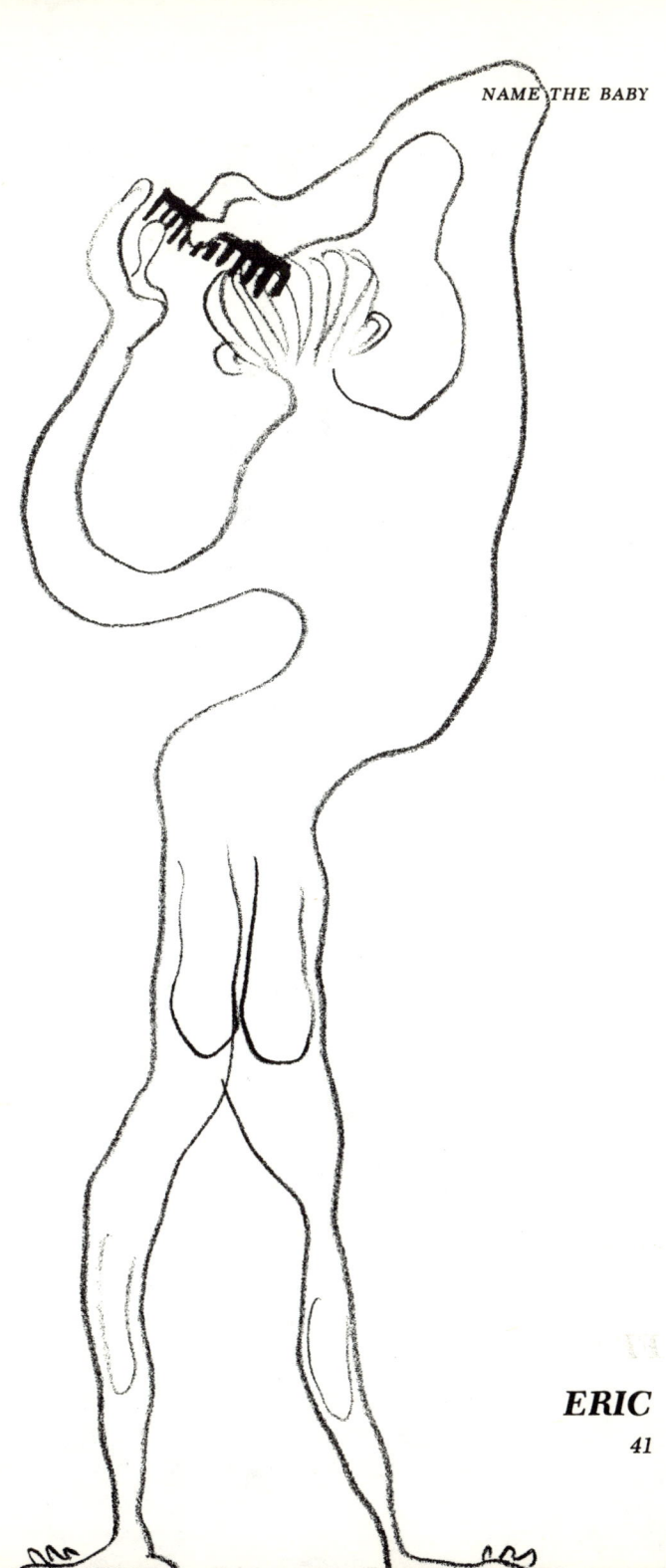

WHAT NOT TO

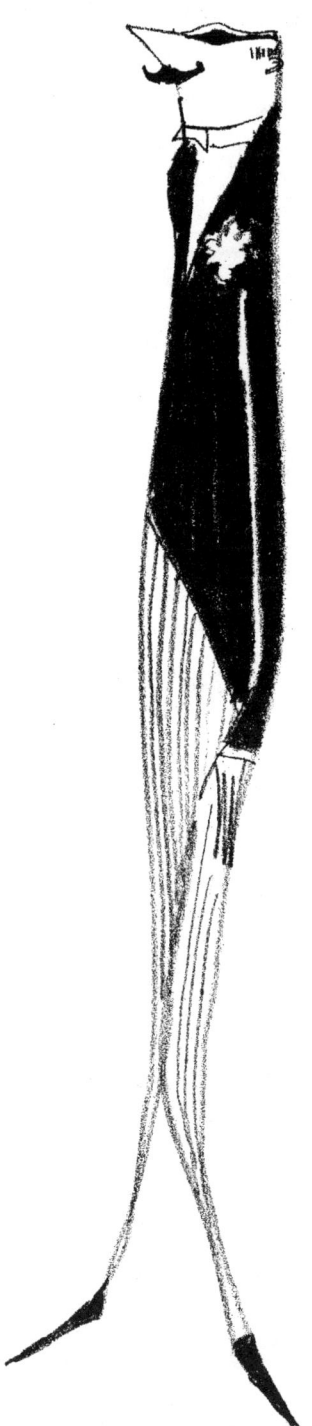

FELIX

FELIX is a bridal consultant. (*See page 42.*)

FRANK—When girls want to redecorate they always get Frank to come over and help them paint or put up wallpaper. He's good at it and doesn't get fresh afterwards. He drinks up all the beer, but he never gets fresh. Frank is always agreeable and polite, but don't get tough with him. He'll kill you.

FRED is skinny and gets his hair cut too high on the sides. He wears striped shirts and works in the same office with Joyce. Fred had a two-week romance once with Valerie and never got over it.

FREDDY is always saying, "Where's the action?" He usually asks Gordie or Dick: They don't know of any action, but pretend they do. The only one who knows where the Action is is Jim and he's there.

WHAT NOT TO

FLETCHER cuts uncancelled stamps off envelopes and saves them.

GAMIAL
See page 125

GARY is spoiled and overweight. Unless he is Gary Cooper.

GAYLORD—Girls think GAYLORD is wonderful because he is so sensitive and is a perfect gentleman and never makes passes or asks them up to his place. GAYLORD is LLOYD's roommate.

GENE is a bachelor who has his TV set in the bedroom and no chairs. Nothing much happens though, because he always gets too interested in the programs.

GEORGE
See page 17

GERALD is a clergyman's son who likes to think he is wicked. He has unexpurgated editions of Henry Miller and photographs of the murals in Pompeii.

GIL—At parties GIL waits until he catches a girl's eye, and then he looks them slowly up

NAME THE BABY

and down with a cute, little smile as if to say "Why, Hel-*oo*, there." If he gets the girl alone, all he can think of to say is "How long have you been in town?" and "Do you like it here better than there?"

GEORGE
See page 125

GLEN goes out with girls and lectures them into bed. Afterwards he criticizes them and tries to change the way they act, dress, and think.

GOOF-BALL
See page 13

GORDON has straight blond hair. He reads a lot and joins a liberal political group in the hope of meeting an intelligent girl he can have a mature relationship with.

GORDIE fancies himself as a Make-out Artist. When he goes out with a girl, he always tells the other fellows all the details of what happened. If nothing happened, he lies about it.

GUS
See page 19

HAL will play the piano at a party if everyone wants to sing.

45

WHAT NOT TO

HAROLD is a friend of HOWARD's.

HARRY
See page 18

HARVEY is the fellow you ask to take your girl someplace when you can't get there until later.

HANK
See page 19

HENRY still wears the eyeglasses with the steel rims they gave him in the army. HENRY is a good fellow to ask to a party. He always brings a bottle, even though he doesn't drink.

HERBERT—Three or four times a year HERBERT writes angry letters to the newspaper complaining about the holes in the streets or the bad service on the buses.

HERB is always looking for a better job or a cheaper apartment.

HERBY is the fellow you ask to wait outside in the hall when you have to go in and see someone. You're always asking HERBY to go someplace with you, but you never take him inside.

HERSCHELL
See page 14

HOMER is the kind of fellow who eats the fortune cookies in a Chinese restaurant. Sometimes he eats the fortunes too.

HORACE says he's going to make a long story short, but doesn't.

HOWARD gets through life okay. It's no strain. He lives in the suburbs, goes to P.T.A. meetings, buys Life Insurance, cheats on his wife once a year and finally buys a Buick. *(See page 48.)*

HOWIE organizes the class reunions and promotes basketball games between the kids and the Old-Timers. HOWIE likes to talk over a P.A. system.

HUBERT tries too hard. He uses antique slang like, " . . . the whole shootin' she– bang . . ."

WHAT NOT TO

HOWARD

HUGHEY used to be an athlete, but he let himself get flabby. He likes to drink beer and sing old school songs, and he has eyes for very young girls. Hughey finally gets into some kind of trouble and no one hears about him anymore.

HY is skinny and scratches a lot. He either talks your head off or has nothing at all to say.

IRVING is always planning big deals. He winds up working for Ben.

ICHABOD—*Ichabod???????*

IRA is sort of jerky but doesn't know it and acts like he was Cary Grant.

IVAN thinks there should be more jokes in *Pravda*.

JACK
See page 18

JAKE is someone's uncle who sends nice presents on Christmas.

WHAT NOT TO

JAMES would like to be like JIM or JIMMY.

JAY is a compulsive check picker upper.

JEFFREY is clean cut and attractive; but he doesn't have a chance. Some girl marries him quick. Usually ROSALIND.

JEROME always finishes what's left on your plate. He acts like he doesn't want to but is doing you a favor.

JERRY has a lot of energy and always has nicks on his face from shaving. JERRY is very big with second-rate girls. After he gets married, he lies about it and keeps putting girls on.

JIM and JIMMY
See page 17

JOE
See page 18

JOEY is a fresh kid brother who won't run errands unless you give him a half dollar.

JOHN
See page 20

JONATHAN likes to refer to himself by his initials.

JULIAN is the Boss. He always has a middle initial, and he's never going to retire.

JULES wears a coat with a velvet collar, drives a big black car and looks like a high-class gangster. He's an accountant.

KENNETH is soft spoken and neat. He was secretly in love with L<small>IZ</small>; but, when he was twenty-six his hair started to fall out, and he married J<small>ANE</small>.

KEN—When your girl goes on to California on a vacation, she meets K<small>EN</small> and marries him.

KENNY is the fellow who helps you move. You don't really know him very well and feel guilty while he's carrying out all the boxes and you keep talking about the big housewarming party you're going to have. But you know that when you have it you'll forget to invite K<small>ENNY</small>.

WHAT NOT TO

KEVIN is a six-year-old boy whose Mother loves him.

KEITH feels he has to live up to his name. He plans to be a mountain climber or live in Acapulco or sail around the world in a thirty-five-foot boat. He ends up in the suburbs.

LANCE
See page 10

LARRY never makes dates until the last minute and, in restaurants, he asks everyone else what they're going to have before he can make up his mind. He once gave up smoking because the clerk said, "What brand?" when he asked for a pack of cigarettes.

LEE works for his father or a successful brother. He has dinner once a week with ARTHUR. They get separate checks.

LEONARD and **LEON** are good card players. They're both successful, LEONARD because he is smart and LEON because he is able to organize other people.

LEN—At parties LEN is always in the kitchen leaning on the refrigerator and holding a can of beer while he talks to some girl. Probably JUNE.

LEO
See page 13

LESLIE knows that there are two c's and one r in occur and that i comes before e except after c.

LESTER worries about germs. He hates to shake hands and gets mad if you breathe on him. He carries a thermometer, has memorized the phone numbers of twelve different doctors, and is the only fellow around who knows what R$_x$ means. His wife always has her purse filled with LESTER's pill bottles; you sometimes wonder what kind of sex life they have.

WHAT NOT TO

LLOYD is an interior decorator. He and GAYLORD live upstairs, and they paint their bathroom black. The neighbors are always complaining about the screaming and door slamming late at night.

LOU
See page 18

LOUIE is well-educated, but is flamboyant and eccentric. Don't go chasing around town late at night with LOUIE or you'll get in trouble. LOUIE won't, but *you* will.

LUCIUS
See page 125

LUTHER—As soon as LUTHER is old enough he buys a Homburg hat. He hates to be called LOU.

LYLE calls up and tells you he is going to commit suicide, and you have to rush over and go out for coffee with him, and he borrows five bucks.

MAC (See SAM)

MAO
See page 125

MAL wishes he were taller and rides a motor scooter. He owns a coat with funny buttons on it and he and MICKEY are buddies.

MARIO plays the accordion. During the Christmas holidays he works part time at the post office.

MARK
See page 18

MARLON keeps taking exercise, but it's no use. He's still getting a pot tummy.

MARTY
See page 19

MARVIN likes to sneak into reserved sections and private beaches. It takes him a long time to get out of the mail room.

MAURICE wears a black hat and never kids around. No one knows what business he's in, but if he wants to he can get you expensive jewelry and good watches wholesale—but really wholesale—MAURICE doesn't try to make a penny off of you.

WHAT NOT TO

MEL never apologizes for burping. He says, "It's a compliment to the cooking." He also drops ashes on the rug and says, "It'll keep the moths out."

MICHAEL is a handsome ten-year-old boy.

MIKE wears a silver identification bracelet and has hairy wrists. MIKE always goes with one girl, but he never talks to her. All anyone ever hears him say at parties is "Okay, honey, let's go home." Later MIKE marries the girl and still never talks to her.

MICKEY—When you have a fight with your girl at a party and walk out on her MICKEY takes her home. MICKEY wears bow ties, and everyone tries to fix him up with PATTY because she's short too. PATTY and MICKEY hate each other.

MILES gets an ulcer.

MITCH has a couple of drinks and he wants to fight.

MONROE—When everyone goes over to MICKEY's house—MICKEY lives with his Mother—and BERNIE puts his feet on the coffee table, MONROE says "Put your feet down, BERNIE, you're not at home now." MONROE is always saying things like "You're not at home now!"

MOOSE was older than the other kids in his grade at school. He got married when he was nineteen and started having children; but he never stays home. He hangs around the school playing ball with the kids.

MORTON is always trying to hypnotize everybody. The only one it ever works on is AUGIE. BERNICE pretends it works on her and talks about how "funny" she felt, but she just wants attention. MORTON doesn't come on with girls at all,

WHAT NOT TO

but GORDIE and GIL are always trying to get MORTON to teach them hypnotism. They figure maybe someday they can get LIZ alone and Wow!

MURRAY has a thin black mustache. When MURRAY dances with a girl he drums on her back with his fingers. (*See page 59.*)

NEAL is someone who belongs to a clique and never pays any attention to you unless he's trying to move in on the girl you brought. If there's a fight at the party, it's NEAL who gets beat up, and everyone is secretly pleased.

NICHOLAS—When NICHOLAS speaks to the waiter in French and orders a special wine, he's not showing off. He's a big spender and a small tipper.

NIKITA
See page 125

NICK
See page 12

NICKY has curly hair and a cute smile and makes out with all the girls GORDIE lies about.

NAME THE BABY

MURRAY

WHAT NOT TO

NORMAN—Some girl gave NORMAN a terrific beating once and he's been afraid to get involved ever since. Keeps saying "Who needs it. I can hire a maid to do everything a wife would do. I come and go as I please." But he's always asking if you know any hustlers.

NORM forgets his glasses and asks if he can borrow your car to go home and get them.

OLIVER carries a pocket slide rule, and his sex life is based on the rhythm system (his own).

OMAR
See page 125

OLLIE—(See page 61.)

OSCAR
See page 18

OSGOOD is a patient, understanding, philosophical father. His wife is expecting their first child in two months.

OTIS wears a belt and suspenders at the same time. He blames his wife for letting him eat so much.

NAME THE BABY

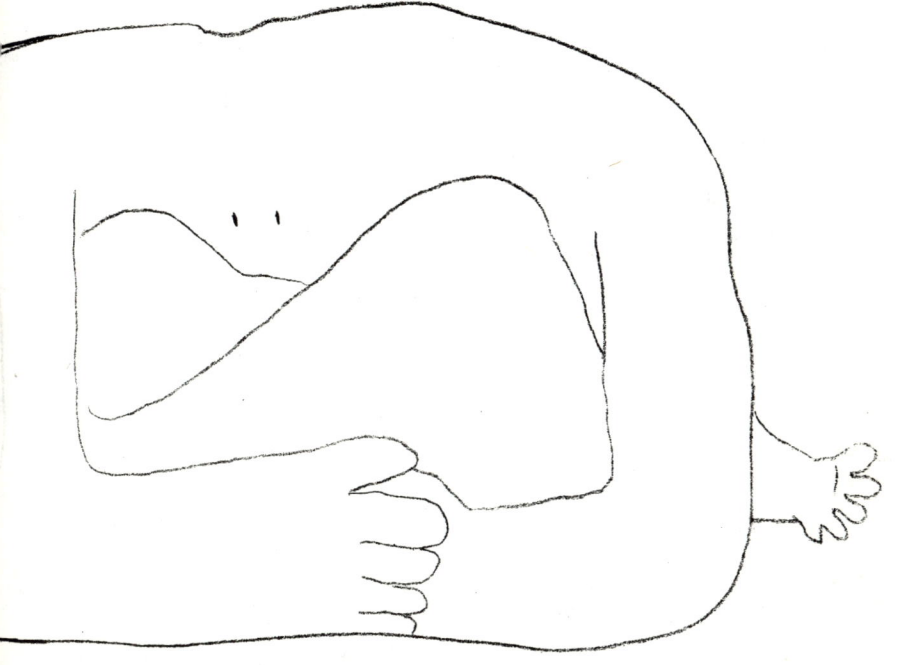

OLLIE

WHAT NOT TO

OWEN wears a truss.

OZZIE takes the dog for a walk as an excuse to get a last drink.

PAUL drives an old car that always has a Coke bottle rolling around on the floor.

PERCY is something like LOUIE, only nuttier. When the Cops come to break up the Party, PERCY gets tough with them and hides their hats.

PETE
See page 19
PETER
See page 19

PHILLIP is a divinity student who talks about religion as if it were basketball. He tells you frankly that he'd like to be a Roman Catholic, but he likes girls too much; so he's going to be an Episcopalian. He ends up in trouble with the law.

PHIL isn't around much. He always has something better to do. He gets married and works for his father-in-law and complains about him. Later he inherits the business, and, when he gets older, he complains about his son-in-law who is working for him.

PORFIRIO
See page 13

QUASIMODO is a bell ringer, with bad posture.

RALPH orders some special, complicated drink and makes a big scene when it isn't fixed right. It's never fixed right; but he keeps ordering it.

RAYMOND is tricky. Don't trust RAYMOND.

RAY is the pal of the fellow who's the leader of the gang. He doesn't like it much when he grows up. He carries an empty brief case back and forth to work.

REX is an old guy who wears bow ties and was a hipster back in 1923.

RICHARD has a dominating Mother and doesn't get along with his Father. He doesn't like DICK either—or very many people.

WHAT NOT TO

RITCHEY was a real hot-shot in school, and you figure he's got to make it. Fifteen years later he calls up, and you're flattered he still remembers you; but he's trying to sell insurance.

ROBERT
See page 20

RONNIE is a charmer and girls fall for him because he cries. He plans to get married as soon as his psychoanalyst tells him it's okay.

ROGER
See page 11

ROLAND has something to do with publishing. (*See page 65.*)

ROSS knows everything. He can settle bets about whether DiMaggio or Williams had the best overall average of runs batted in.

ROVER should stay off the sofa.

ROY—There are two kinds of Roys, the Big City Roy and the Small Town Roy. The Big City Roy has a fat face and his ambition is to be the best used-car salesman in

NAME THE BABY

ROLAND

town. He's always standing out front next to the lemon they have up on the platform as the "Daily Special" and jingling coins and keys in his pocket. The Small Town Roy has a big adam's apple and hollow cheeks. He's the one who buys the "Daily Special."

RUDY is fat, wears a pinky ring, and uses terrible language. He has a friend who's a thief and who can get you *anything*.

RUSS—Things happen to Russ. He's always having a wreck, or breaking his big toe, or getting his shirt caught in his zipper.

SAM—Everyone in the world is named Sam. They just don't know it.

SEYMOUR—Anyone who is constantly called Seymour is in trouble.

SHELLY wonders whether or not he should grow a beard.

SHEP is okay. He's sort of a hip **HOWARD**.

SHORTY isn't very tall.

SMILEY is a racket guy who has a scar running from his right ear to the left side of his chin.

SOCRATES—Only a dominating or frustrated Father could give a child an outrageous name such as **SOCRATES** or **ALGERNON** or **ARISTOTLE**. This child will do badly in school and wind up being presented with a gold watch after working twenty-five years at the same unimportant job —unless, of course, he happens to be a Greek. Then **SOCRATES** is an okay name and when the child grows up he will, no doubt, continue to be a Greek. As to being important—there is no such thing as an unimportant Greek.

STANLEY believes that a really smart operator can always take an Idea and parlay it into a million bucks. By the time STANLEY is thirty years old the only thing he's really big at is smoking.

STAN talks a lot about MG's and Alfa Romeo's and Porsche 1600's; but he drives a 1954 Chevy.

STEVE likes controversy. He has a lot of odd information about odd subjects and is always making out big lists.

STEWIE acts like a big man till his Mother gets there. Later, he acts like a big man till his wife gets there.

SY—Girls are always teaching SY to dance. He smiles a lot and never loses his temper. SY doesn't look tough; but he had a good combat record in the war. SY likes PATTY; but she thinks he's not going to amount to anything and brushes him off. Later, when SY is very successful,

NAME THE BABY

PATTY keeps telling her husband, who isn't, how SY was crazy about her and wanted to marry her.

TECUMSEH
See page 125

TED is husky and nice-looking and girls think he is deep because he doesn't talk much—but it's only because he can't think of anything to say. He marries the girl he took to the Senior Prom.

TEDDY is your girl's sixteen-year-old brother who wears Ivy League clothes and treats you like you were a Russian spy with halitosis.

TOM
See page 17

TIM is a bartender and is a friend of AGGIE's. About once a month he closes up an hour early and goes home with AGGIE. For the next week, AGGIE doesn't come in the place.

TONY
See page 17

TINY is a fat man with a little nose and little feet and a lot of hair.

ULYSSES
See page 125

69

VICTOR always impresses you when you see him. He looks shrewd, tough, intelligent, efficient. When you have to go to court for anything; VICTOR is always the other fellow's lawyer. Your lawyer is a cousin of HERBY's who still has the same brief case he used in college.

VINCENT has all of his clothes tailor-made and makes terrible puns.

VINCE gives the impression he's wearing a shoulder holster.

WALDO is a dude. He wishes it were still okay to wear pointed, yellow shoes, and double-breasted vests.

WALLACE hangs around museums because he figures he can meet lonely out-of-town girls. It worked once.

NAME THE BABY

WALTER—There are several different kinds of WALTERS. The only thing they have in common is that none of them is WALT or WALLY.

WALT is chunky and wears glasses and hangs around drinking with ALFRED, NICKOLAS, and MIKE. WALT does well in the world, but does badly with girls. He likes them, but when he gets around a first class girl he kicks his feet and tells dumb jokes.

WALLY used to save stamps; but now he has a lathe in the basement and does woodworking. He reads science fiction and *Popular Mechanics* and likes to get on mailing lists.

WARREN—When WARREN takes a girl out he is thoughtful, considerate, reserved, never makes suggestive remarks, and gives the impression that he has a large private income. The girl thinks she has

WHAT NOT TO

struck gold; but on the third date, all of a sudden, he turns into a sex-crazed monster. (*See page 73.*)

WENDELL is never doing as well now as he used to.

WHITEY, BUCK or MOOSE
See page 14

WILBUR hangs around chain drug stores and when girls stop to look at the Pocket Books, he sidles up to them and says, "Say, I bet you like to read a lot." He gets arrested.

WILLIAM
See page 20

WOODROW
See page 18

NAME THE BABY

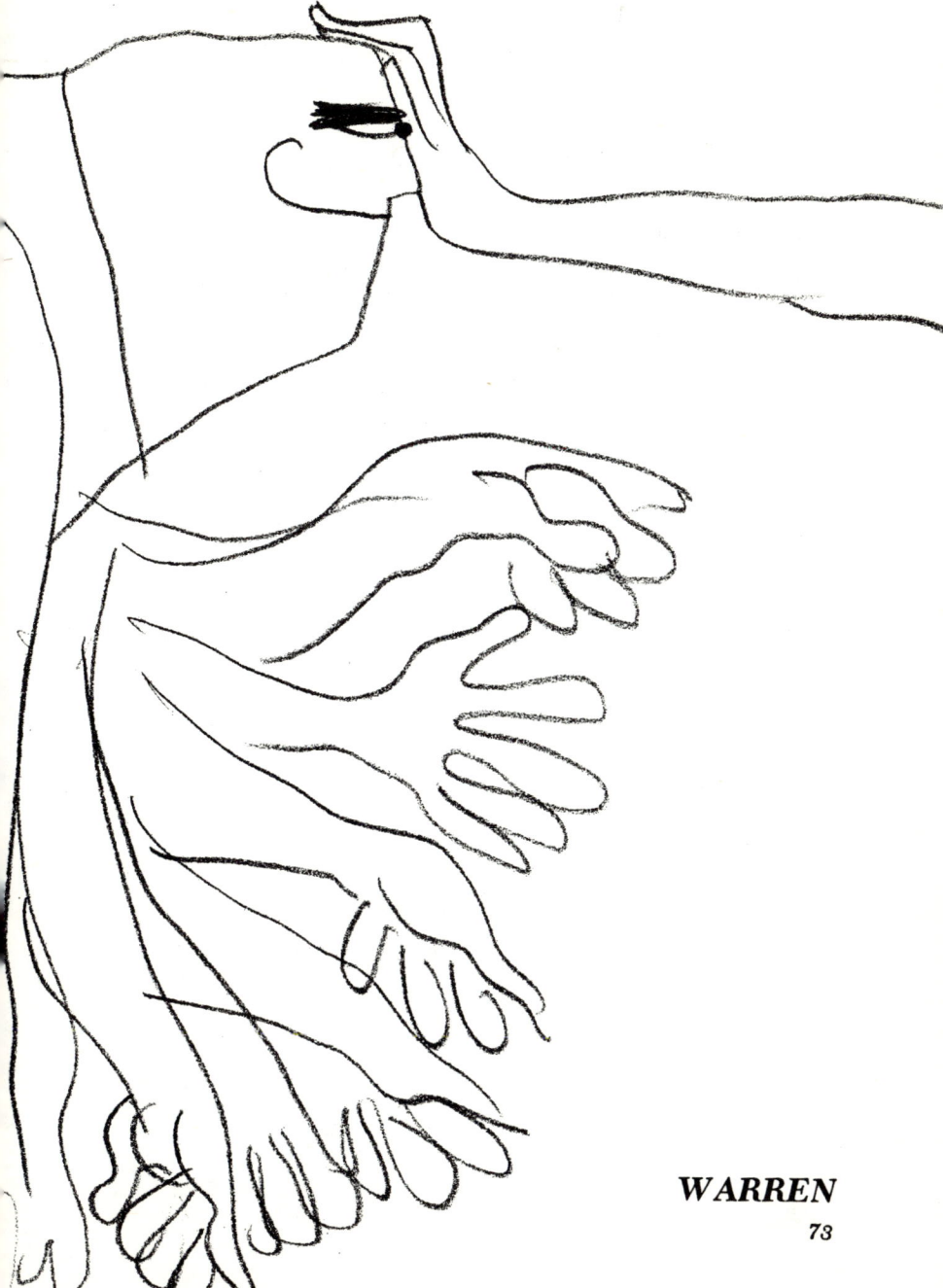

WARREN

Girls and also Women:

AGATHA
See page 16

AGNES wears Oxfords with inch and a half heels and is always complaining about the terrible "smutty" novels they publish nowadays and describing the "disgusting" scenes she objects to.

AGGIE has a couple of neighborhood bars she hangs out in. She has long discussions with the other Regulars about How Whales Mate or Can Dogs Really Think, stuff like that. When AGGIE comes to a party she usually leaves alone. (*See page 75.*)

ALICE—As they get older the other suburban wives get irritated with ALICE because she eats everything and doesn't get fat.

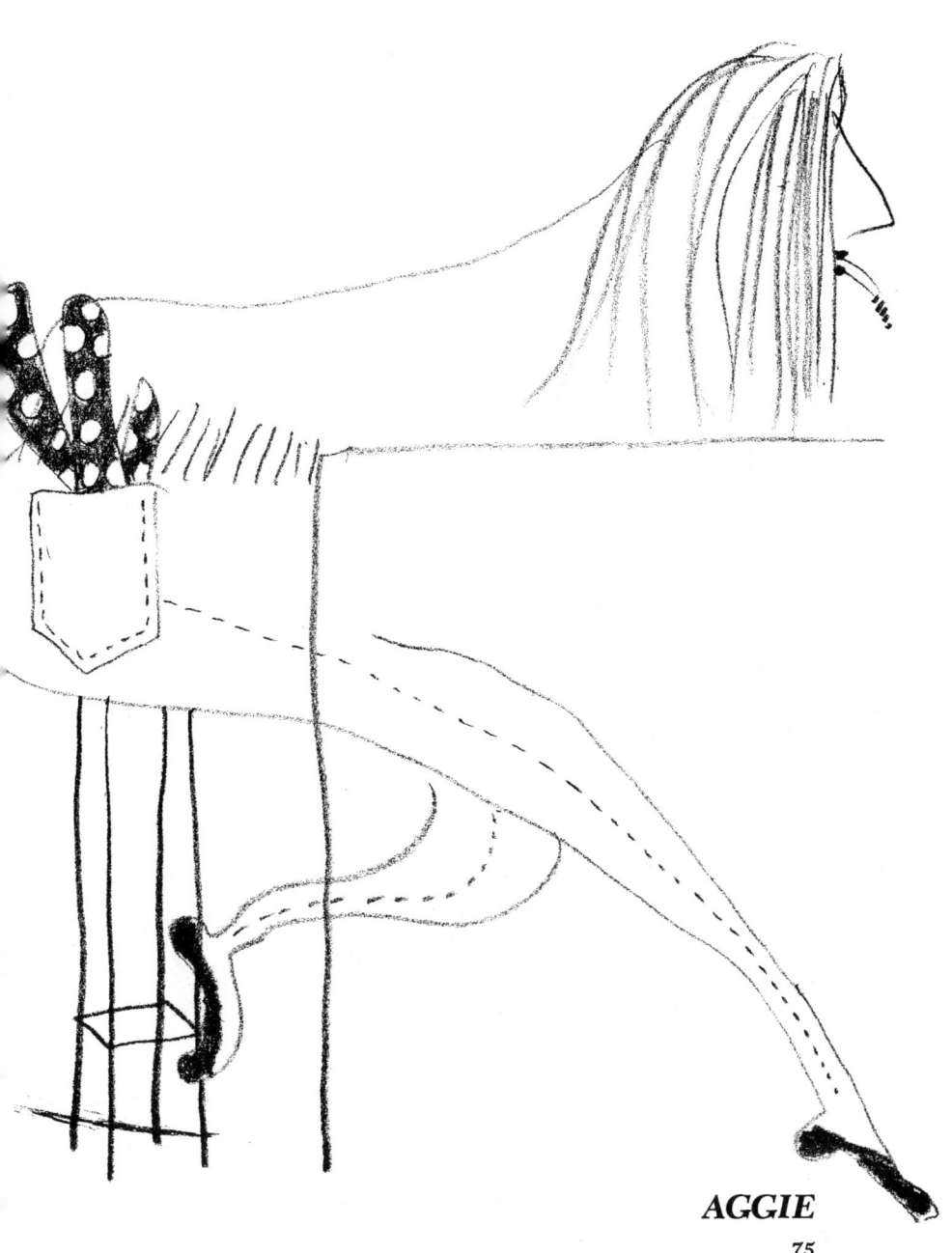

WHAT NOT TO

ALMA is an ex-WAC who owns her own bowling ball.

AMANDA and **ANNIE** are either plain, friendly girls or they are Knock Outs and are in show business. (*See page 77.*)

ANN
See page 21

ANITA looks sort of foreign. She's the kind of a girl other women use the word "stunning" about. ANITA marries NICKY, but it doesn't last. After that NICKY falls apart, but ANITA looks better than ever.

ARLENE
See page 15

AUDREY gives the impression she's interested in Action. But she isn't. Guys can't understand that the trouble isn't them—and they keep trying.

BARBARA lives in the suburbs with HOWARD.

BERNICE is an attractive girl's friend or roommate. BERNICE has long hair, wears tight

76

NAME THE BABY

AMANDA and **ANNIE**

belts, and uses depilatory on her arms. She telephones fellows.

BERYL is pretty and very sweet, but for some reason or other you feel sorry for her.

BETTE
See page 17

BESS is active in a religious organization. She also reads palms.

BETTINA—You think BETTINA wears falsies until you see her in a bathing suit. Unbelievable.

BETTY LOU—Unless BETTY LOU is southern (many double names are southern and properly belong in another survey which might be titled, "What Not to Name Your-alls Baby"), she marries someone her family doesn't approve of and goes to live in Levittown.

BEVERLY tosses her hair and laughs a lot.

BEV is soft spoken. You can make out with **BEV** if you don't rush her.

BILLIE's slip is usually showing, but it doesn't bother her much.

B.J. (for *Barbara Jo, Betty Jane,* etc.)—Girls called B.J. insist on being called B.J. They are smart and attractive and make excellent executive secretaries. It's hard to get a date with B.J. When you call, she's always just going someplace for the weekend or just getting back; but she says she really wants to see you and please call her again. B.J. eventually marries a nice fellow in the office.

BLANCHE is always yanking her kids by the collar and yelling, "Put that down!" and "What's the matter with you?" The kids don't answer. When they get older **BLANCHE** stops yanking them by the collar and says, "Don't talk to me like that. Who do you think you are anyway!" The kids still don't answer. They're still trying to figure out what's the matter with them.

BOBBY chews gum and saves pictures of Tony Curtis.

BONNIE is a living doll. She smells sensational and the fellows who kissed BONNIE in high school never forget it. Every so often, for the rest of their lives, they think of BONNIE and wonder what might have happened if. . . . Once in a while one of these fellows looks up BONNIE and before he sees her he tells himself he's foolish and that twenty-five years have passed and she must be frumpy and ordinary looking by now and she probably never really was very much. Then he meets her and BONNIE is still the greatest. He feels lousy for about a month.

CANDY is either a little kid or a stripper.

CARLOTTA
See pages 10 and 15

NAME THE BABY

CATHY is always getting sick or just getting over something. She leaves early because she has to get to bed.

CAROL
See page 15

CATHERINE
See page 20

CEIL lives for her eight-year-old daughter who takes dancing and singing lessons. Ceil is always quoting the things the daughter says.

CHRISTINE
See page 16

CLARA
See page 15

CLEO is the one who squeezes all the chocolates in a box trying to find the ones with the liquid cherry centers.

CONNIE
See page 17

CORA carries a huge shoulder-strap bag that has everything in it from shoes to turtle food.

CYNTHIA is very feminine. Other girls don't trust Cynthia. She marries a fellow she thinks has money—Tom or maybe Christopher—and gets up every morning before he wakes and puts on lipstick and ties a ribbon in her hair.

DARLENE is a hillbilly who once won a beauty contest.

WHAT NOT TO

DAISY — (See page 83.)

DEBBY is a teen-ager.

DENISE is wholesome. That is, unless she's French. If she's French—she's French.

DEEDY or **DEEDIE** has well-to-do parents. They buy her a terrific car.

DIANE or **DIANA** gives the impression that she is interested in action. And she is. She has beautiful hands and is proud of them.

DIEDRE is a rotten five-year-old, who's always snitching on the other kids.

DORIS is attractive and friendly, but, if you try to kiss her, she perspires and won't stop talking.

NAME THE BABY

DAISY

WHAT NOT TO

DOTTIE brings home stray cats. Her roommate brings home stray fellows. The cats last longer than the fellows.

EDITH can't do enough for her daughter, HOPE. She picks out her furniture, buys her china and her dresses. If HOPE ever gets mad at her husband and wants to go home to Mama, it's right next door.

EDNA is pretty and has tremendous energy. She's fun at parties and is always organizing something. When she decides to get married, she picks out someone, and he doesn't have a chance.

EILEEN
See page 16

ELAINE is dark and intense and is very serious about going to an analyst. If you can convince ELAINE you're off your rocker, or, at least, "disturbed," you've got it made. But she's pretty sharp and it's best not to try this unless you *are* a little nutty to begin with.

ELLEN makes artificial flowers. She has a little kit. She tried to sell them, but couldn't; now she makes them and gives them to her friends who tell her she should try to sell them.

ELLY is always knitting socks for her boy friend; but, by the time the socks are finished, she's broken up with him. She has a drawer full of assorted sizes.

ELIZABETH
See page 21

ELSIE always looks like she's on the way to the dentist's.

EMILY has "dates" with her Daddy. She is Daddy's girl. She and Daddy are "real pals." Daddy tries to be jolly; but you can see he doesn't really care too much for the fellows in EMILY's crowd.

EMMA was captain of the field hockey team in school. She charges through life like an army tank. Later she may take in foster children.

WHAT NOT TO

ETHEL failed her driver's test four times. When ETHEL goes to the Laundromat, she always jams the machine.

EVELYN wears brown and empties ash trays.

EVE is so nice that no one notices that she is really a plain, gawky sort of girl.

FAY puts peroxide on her own hair; but not often enough. She likes to ride on the back of motorcycles, and she'll lend fellows money—if she has any.

FLORENCE
See page 19

FRANCES—Last summer FRANCES drove to California in a Volkswagen with three other girls. FRANCES owns fifteen shares of G.M. stock.

FRAN is a friend of DEWEY's.

FREIDA is always scrubbing the floors and then putting newspapers over them.

GAIL is graceful and a slow talker who is pleased if people ask her if she is from the south.

GAY isn't.

GEORGIA
See page 16

GERALDINE is a lovely girl who always seems younger than she is.

GERRY—When Gerry was a kid, she used to climb trees and play baseball—later, she played golf and tennis. When fellows would try to kiss her, she would slap them. Finally, one fellow slapped her back and broke her nose. She married him.

GERTRUDE, TRUDY or GERT
See page 15

GINGER is a drag.

GINNY is a Kittenish Divorcée. She always has a lot of pictures of herself around the house. (*See page 88.*)

GLADYS talks you into coming to a "simply fabulous" party she's having and when you show up there are seven people there who don't know each other, and Gladys serves canned spaghetti and garlic bread.

GLORIA buys drapes.

GOOGIE—There are a group of wealthy (not rich, but wealthy) people who spend summers in the Hamptons and winter in Palm Beach or Cap d'Antibes. These people waste the first half of their day planning how they're going to waste the second half. Their biggest problem is Which Car Shall We Take and they give themselves names as foolish as the lives they lead. Names like GOOGIE, SUSU, BOBO, TOTO, BINKY, BUFFY, etc. An interesting example of the Theory of Names. (*See page 90.*)

GRETCHEN's boy friends are always leaving her to go back to their wives.

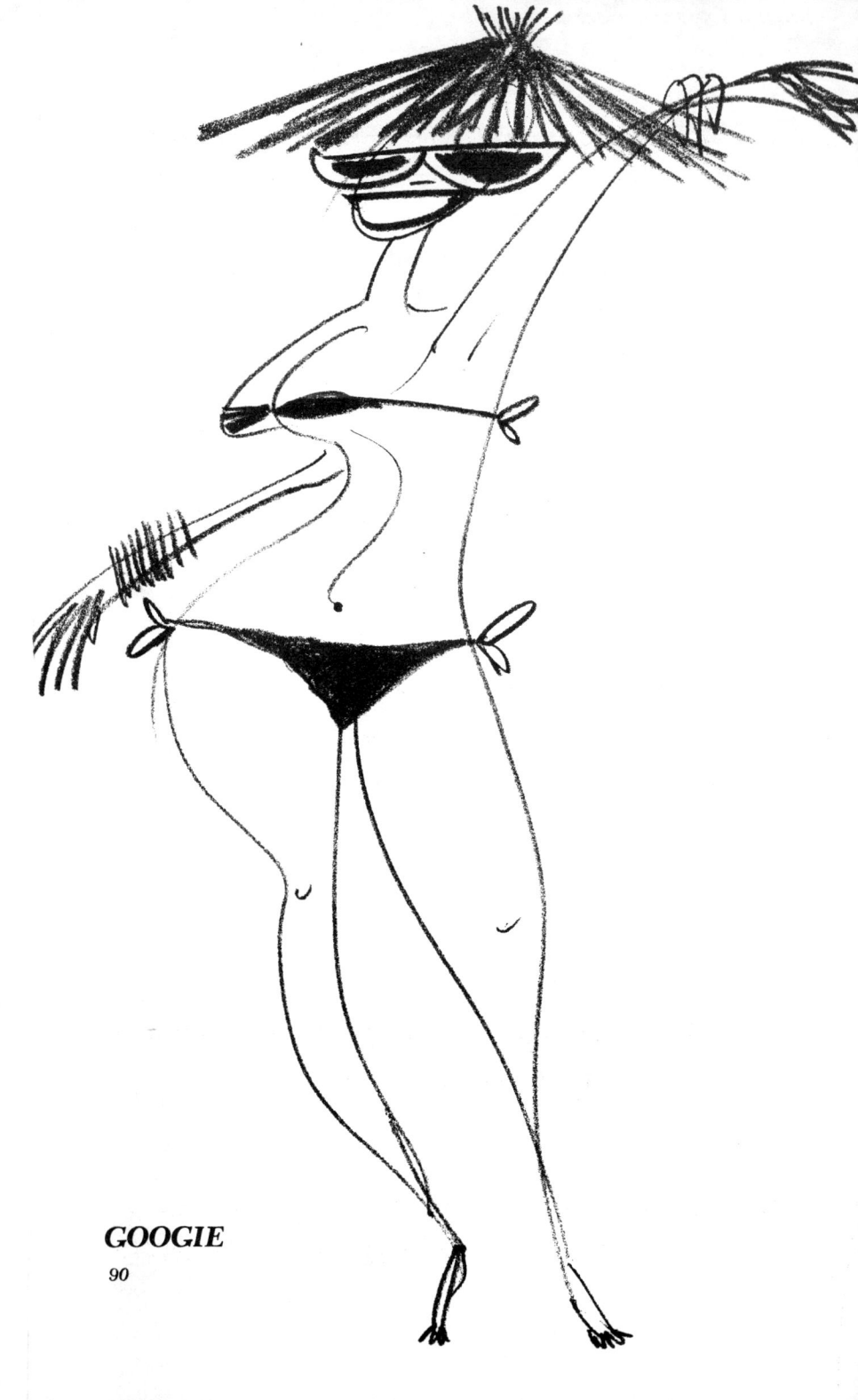

GOOGIE

GRACE buys nice furniture and then puts plastic slip covers over it. She also keeps the blinds pulled down all day so the sun won't bleach her rugs. Her husband never brings home a friend without letting her know twenty-four hours in advance.

HARRIET tells everyone that she is a virgin. No one cares much.

HAZEL is chunky. She buys a fox jacket which makes her look chunkier.

HELEN
See page 15

HOLLY follows a fellow clear across the country and marries him.

HONEY is very small and is always running around carrying something.

HOPE—Her Mother takes HOPE on a cruise so she can meet an eligible fellow. HOPE meets one and he marries her. The next year HOPE, the fellow, and her Mother go on a cruise.

IRENE wanted to be a buyer for a big store, but she quit and married DICK. She dyes streaks in her hair, is long legged and well-groomed. IRENE is a good cook but a bad housekeeper.

IRMA
See page 16

ISABEL has a round little figure and is maternal. Everyone loves ISABEL except the fellow she's hung up on. He's a nut.

INGRID has rosy cheeks and big feet.

JACKIE
See page 16

JAN is a rebel. She's also touchy.

JANE
See page 15

JANET was a camp counselor. No one is quite sure whether JANET swings or not. If she does, she's very cool about it.

JOAN
See page 15

JOSEPHINE is the big center on the girls' basketball team. She compensates for her size by being, what ELAINE would call, "permissive" with fellows—but only if they're six inches shorter than she is.

JOYCE has seniority in the office typing pool.

JUDITH is impressed by people. She keeps talking about the time she once met Norman Bel Geddes.

JUDY
See page 16

JULIE has the lead in the school play.

JUNE is pretty and knows it. She has shoulder-length blond hair and wears pinafores.

JOANNA is a natural blonde who comes on big with any fellow who seems to be showing an interest in another girl. Once she gets the fellow's attention, she cuts out and starts up with someone else. JOANNA doesn't have many girl friends.

KAY is a tall nervous girl who wears suits and bites her false fingernails. She marries HAROLD or ALEX.

KIM is a three-year-old kid who bites.

KITTY is always buying clothes and adding things. She gets a dress and sews on a little pocket with a ribbon or some cloth flowers. When she buys a scarf, she sews sequins all over it.

LAURA
See page 16

LAURIE is someone's kid sister. The boys always treat her like a sister. At a party she decides she'll get drunk and maybe something will happen. But she just gets sick.

LEE is a successful career girl. She is very feminine and charming. A lot of married

NAME THE BABY

men she works with are in love with LEE. They never get anywhere; but they keep hoping.

LEONORE, LENORA, and LEONA are lonesome. Men take them out; but they never bring them presents.

LIL
See page 15

LILY or LILLY is cool. There's something exotic about LILY and she's considered very sexy by a lot of people, including herself. She has an ornate, ultrafeminine bedroom. LILY never goes to fellows' apartments; but if she digs you she'll insist you come in for a nightcap. Wow!

LILLIAN
See page 15

LINDA is someone's fifteen-year-old daughter who shouldn't be left alone with her father's friends.

LISA is a girl who spends a lot of time saying ". . . . With an S, not a Z."

WHAT NOT TO

LIZ is beautiful, sensual, and a good sport, which is quite a parley.

LOLITA should get in earlier.

LORETTA has a lot of curly hair and works in the office with Joyce, Eleanor, Marge and Donna. Once a week they all have dinner out together and get into a friendly argument over the check. They all wear inexpensive blouses, buy sling-back shoes at a chain store, and try all the new shades of lipstick and nail polish. After dinner they often go to a dance hall. Loretta is the best looking in this group. Donna is the heaviest. (*See page 97.*)

LOUISE
See page 15

LORRAINE takes guitar lessons and goes to a Writing Class once a week. She wants to *fulfill* herself and insists that men respect her as an individual. She's a pushover if you talk to her for twenty minutes about Adlai Stevenson or Proust. (*See page 98.*)

WHAT NOT TO

LORRAINE

NAME THE BABY

LUCILLE usually looks like she's smelling something and is trying to figure out what it is. (*See page 101.*)

LUCY still wears a page-boy hairdo. She is willowy and girls think she is pretty; but fellows never take her out more than twice.

MABEL—When the fellows get together in one corner of the room and tell dirty jokes, MABEL gets close enough to hear them. Then when the other girls giggle and say, "Aren't they awful. What'd they say?" MABEL says, "Never mind, I'll tell you later."

MADELINE
See page 15

MARGARET
See page 20

MARGE—There are two kinds. One MARGE works in the Office with JOYCE and is always kidding about wanting a date. She says she likes men and doesn't care what type "so long as they're breathing." When LORETTA's boy friend does get her a date, she puts on too much make-up and then gets sore if the guy

WHAT NOT TO

MARION
See page 19

MARYANE
See page 17

tries to put his arm around her. The other MARGE has small hips and nice legs and wears toreador pants with high heels and a lot of junk jewelry. She is a good drinker, but never shows it. She is popular and people are always stopping by. (*See page 103.*)

MAUREEN has broad shoulders, slender legs, and freckles on her chest. MAUREEN is very big with kissing.

MAXINE was the only girl in High School who went out with a married man. Later she got married. Then she started going out with single guys.

MILDRED gets hay fever every September.

MILI
See page 17

MIMI—No one can ever remember what MIMI's husband does or what he looks like.

MING TOY
See page 20

MURIEL is always telling you about men following her on the street. She keeps her

NAME THE BABY

LUCILLE

window locked at night and carries a beer-can opener in her bag for protection. MURIEL has soft eyes and a long neck and lots of fellows go for her; but, actually, she's not interested. She is always trying to change her name to "NICOLE" or "ONDINE" but everyone keeps calling her MURIEL. If something happens and she does have an affair with someone, she's liable to wind up with a nervous breakdown.
(*See page 105.*)

MYRTLE started keeping a diary, but after three years the only things she had in it were notes on movies she'd seen and her appointments with the dentist to have her braces adjusted. So she burned it.

NANCY lives in a nice suburb and has a nice husband, a nice barbecue pit, a nice den, and a nice station wagon. She is the prettiest wife on their street and the other husbands have eyes for her; but NANCY is loyal and never cheats.

NAME THE BABY

MARGE

She flirts a little, but she never cheats. Or at least, if she does cheat, no one ever knows about it, which, looking at it from NANCY's point of view, is the same thing.

NATALIE is a talker. You ask NATALIE how she is—she tells you. (*See page 109.*)

NAOMI is voluptuous and is always putting blue polish on her nails or wearing adhesive tape instead of a bra or sprinkling glitter in her hair or showing up in a slit-to-the-waist blouse. She scares the bejezis out of most fellows, but AUGIE likes her. But then AUGIE likes everyone.

NORMA
See page 16

OLIVIA shows up at a party with a dress that's cut too low and keeps asking the fellows if they think her dress is cut too low.

PAMELA is slender and flat-chested and wears sandals and Bohemian clothes; but she

104

MURIEL

never hangs around Bohemian places or with far-out people. PAMELA works for a trade magazine called the *Foot Digest*. She has the title of Assistant Managing Editor and gets seventy-four dollars a week. She is always about to marry some advertising executive; but it never happens. You can score with PAMELA if you take her seriously, but you know how it is with some girls you're sorry the next day. With PAMELA you're sorry while it's going on.

PAM's Mother goes out with her a lot. PAM's Mother has bleached hair and is almost as much fun as PAM, which isn't much. PAM's Father tries to be a good fellow —he's a lot older than PAM's Mother— and he invites the fellows in the gang to come over and use the pool table in the basement. He doesn't really want them there though.

PATRICIA, PAT, PATSY, PATTY
See page 19

PATTY is something like JACKIE only PATTY has a smaller chest and bigger hips.

PAULINE is thin and dark.

PEARL is shy and quiet, unless she comes from a farm. Then she's shy and noisy.

PEGGY
See page 16

PENNY—About eleven o'clock PENNY's Father telephones to remind her that it's getting late and she goes home. PENNY's Father is the kind of man who keeps whiskey in glass bottles labeled "Scotch" and "Bourbon." Every once in a while he holds one of the bottles up to the light, looks at it and then says, "Mother" (he calls his wife, "Mother"). He says, "Mother, we'd better get another bottle of Bourbon." They buy one bottle at a time.

PHYLLIS is the last girl in town you'd ever expect to get "in trouble." She manages somehow.

POLLY—There was a time when everyone thought POLLY was the greatest thing that ever happened. But, somehow, she never made it.

PRUDENCE—Girls named Prudence, Charity or Patience are pushovers.

QUANDRA—Odd or far-out names, like Quandra, Elmarie, Imelda, Haralda, Fleur, Zenobia, etc., indicate the girl will be some sort of odd or far-out type. She'll probably end up in New York and may become a little Beat. She'll certainly wear leotards around the house and own a lot of black clothes. (*See page 114*.)

REBECCA is beautiful. Becky is someone's grandmother.

RHOADA wears a flashy hairdo, all piled on one side, usually, and pastes a false beauty spot on her cheek. She thinks she is exotic; but too much of her gums show when she smiles. Rhoada goes out with

NAME THE BABY

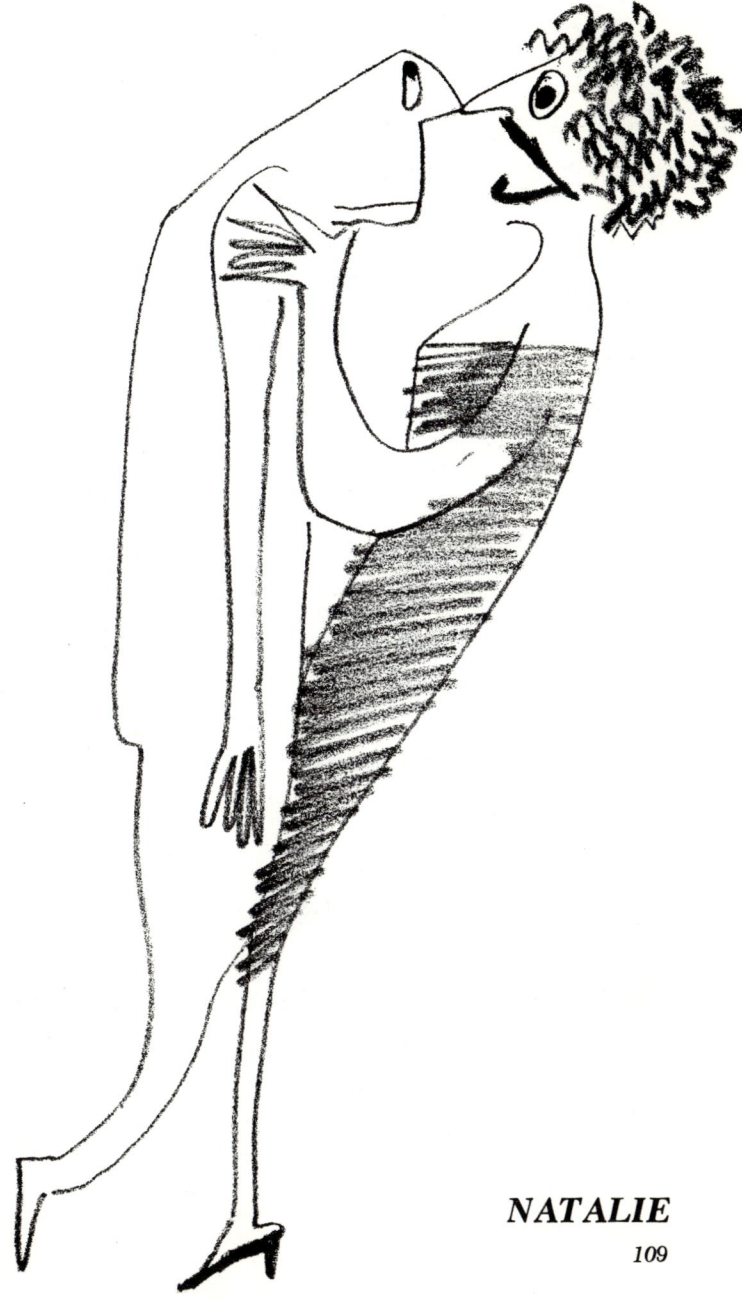

NATALIE

WHAT NOT TO

bald-headed older men who look like they're from out of town and who smell like a barber shop. They take her to small night spots that feature 40-watt bulbs and circulating violin players. She finally marries some of these men and the high point of her life is when she gets her picture in the paper during one of the divorces.

RITA
See page 14

ROBERTA is tallish and dark and makes noises when men touch her. The fellows get pretty impressed at first; but then they begin to wonder if she's putting it on.

ROBIN is a name a girl gives herself. She is aggressive and given to telling fanciful tales about her family and her past. Don't get mixed up with ROBIN.

ROSALIND says she wants "a man who will dominate me," but she never finds one. A lot of fellows make out with ROSALIND on the second or third date; then she won't see them anymore. Makes the fellows pretty nervous. NICKY was the only one who didn't figure there was something wrong with him. ROSALIND finally marries someone who is scared of her and tries to manage his life.

ROZ is the same as ROSALIND.

ROSE goes to the powder room with the other girls and cuts up the fellow she is with.

ROSEMARY is very female. She is the kind of a girl fellows should marry; but they don't realize it until they're trapped with CYNTHIA or AUDREY.

SALLY—What ever became of Sally?

SANDRA has to have her own way or she gets mad. SANDRA has one plain-looking friend who is very loyal to her.

WHAT NOT TO

SANDI worries about getting too much sun.

SARAH has a good job and her own apartment. She has a long time romance going with MAURICE. He never gets there until after ten o'clock and never takes her out.

SELMA always has a hard-luck story.

SHEILA likes to read Russian novels and go to sad movies.

SHERRY is as cute as a kitten and has a lovely, trim figure. She is also neat and friendly and goes out of her way to do favors. SHERRY never flirts or acts like she is interested in action—but she makes DIANE seem like an amateur.

SHIRLEY still believes that, somehow or other, Eddie Fisher and Debbie Reynolds will get back together again.

SIS has to take care of her Mother so she becomes an art teacher in grade school.

SUE swings.

SUSAN
See page 14

SYLVIA is very hippy, but you don't notice because she has excellent posture and great taste in clothes. SYLVIA has silver-blond hair and no one makes out with her. It's not because SYLVIA isn't sexy. It's just that she doesn't want to get mussed up.

TALLULAH
See page 125

TERESA is ANTHONY's sister. She has thick, bushy hair and is the only one who never cheats in school. When the Teacher leaves the room and says, "No talking while I'm gone," TERESA is the only one who doesn't talk.

TERI
See page 17

TERRY is divorced and supports a small child by working nights in a restaurant or night club. You only ask TERRY for a date if

WHAT NOT TO

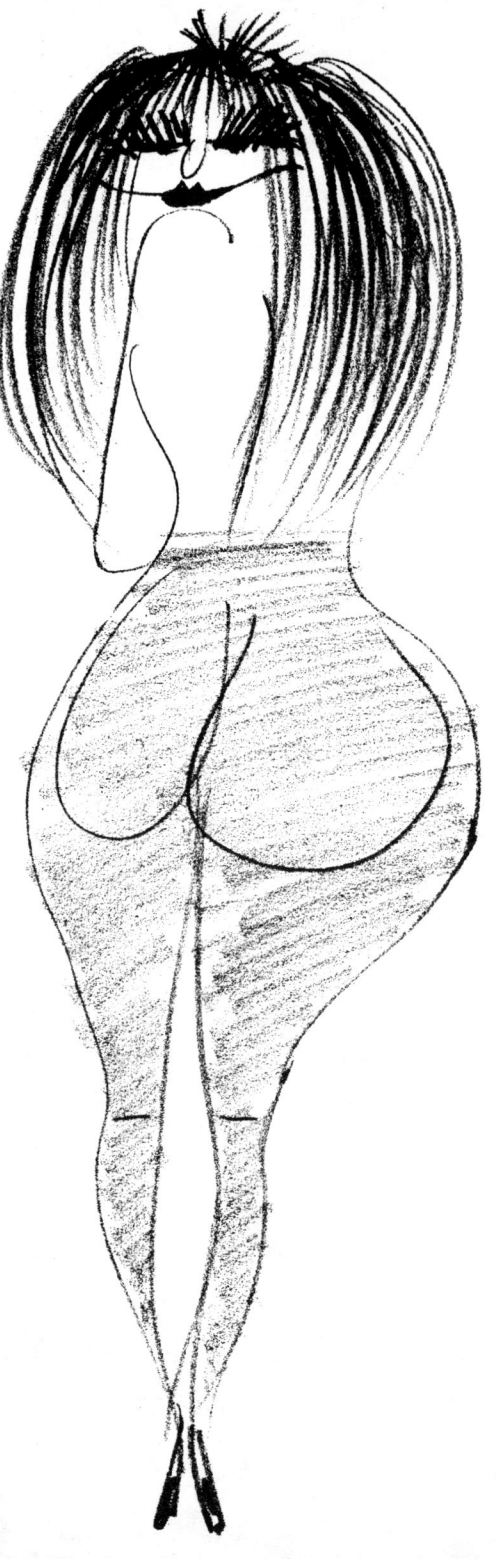

QUANDRA

114

you're desperate. Not because she isn't pretty; but because you have the feeling that she won't show up. You're usually right.

THELMA orders hot-fudge sundaes with whipped cream and then puts saccharine in her coffee.

TRACEY—Girls who have been given family surnames for first names like TRACEY, HUDSON, KELLY, STACEY, etc. can swear or use bad language and no one minds.

VALERIE uses men to get ahead.

VERA is jealous of her husband and puts him down in public.

VERONICA—At nineteen VERONICA is a stunning hat-check girl. At twenty-five she is a movie starlet. At thirty-one she is a stunning hat-check girl.

WHAT NOT TO

VI manages to get married. No one can figure out how.

VICKI designs and makes her own clothes.

VIOLA
See page 16

VIRGINIA washes her hair every Saturday morning and puts a turban on over her pin curls and goes shopping. Virginia's conversation consists mostly of complaints about her permanent, or discussions of television shows or movies. She may get plump, but she never seems to really grow up. Virginia isn't unhappy. She has a couple of loyal boy friends, Augie and Stan, and it never occurs to her not to let them stay over.

VIVIAN is lively but choosy. She is a selective swinger and picks out fellows she likes. Old boy friends are always trying to start up again with Vivian; but she never makes the same scene twice.

WILMA is usually pregnant. She goes downtown in her eighth month wearing slacks. She hates Dr. Spock.

WINIFRED's parents weren't too well off; but she makes a "good marriage" and spends the rest of her life complaining about her maid.

WINNIE is the one you get your out-of-town friends a date with when they say "Hey, you're a big operator around here. Fix me up with a lively broad." WINNIE always comes through and makes you a Big Man. If you know a WINNIE, keep on her good side and don't louse it up by making a pass at her yourself. She's a godsend.

YVONNE
See page 16

ZELDA picks out a movie star to look like. She always picks out Audrey Hepburn and somehow she never *quite* makes it. (See page 118.)

ZSA ZSA
See page 125

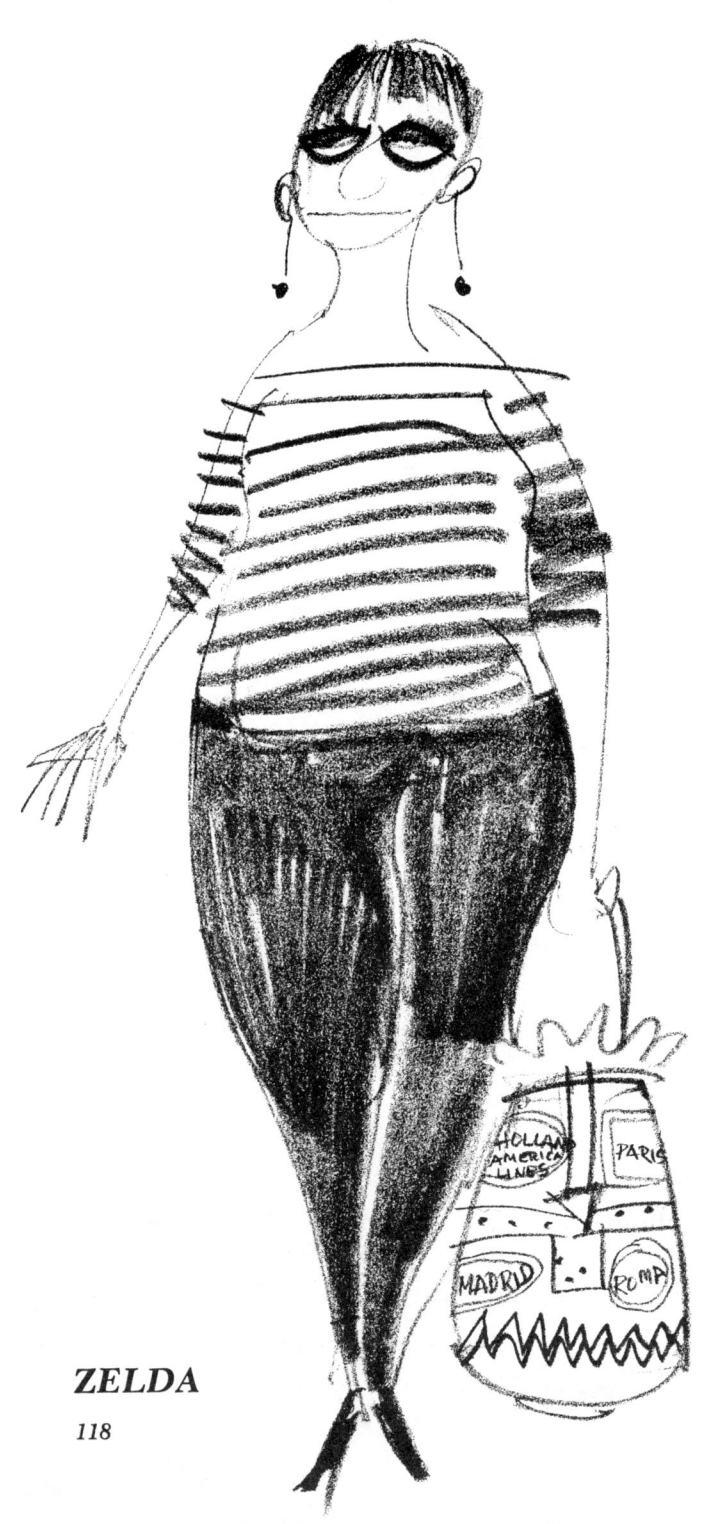

ZELDA

DO IT YOURSELF

At this point, you may find that you disagree with some—or all—of our findings regarding names. If so, remember that, because of the high cost of electronic computers, this book was compiled by low-cost humans who are entitled to make a few errors.

One of the errors was winding up with an oversupply of Types without names. We had originally planned to sweep them under an Editor and walk quietly away, but instead we have decided to give you a chance to get even. Simply fill in the name of whoever fits. In other words, do it yourself.

NAME   MALES

_____ phones at 2 a.m. and says, "Did I wake you up?"

_____ carries around two-year-old newspaper clippings that mention his name.

WHAT NOT TO

NAME   MALES

_____ is an unsuccessful wolf.

_____ is a successful wolf.

_____ is usually very quiet, but, after a couple of drinks, he will tell you long, sad stories about his life.

_____ should see his dentist twice a week, at least.

_____ looks like the one who writes rude things on the walls in public places. (No one sees him, but you know he is the one.)

_____ takes ten minutes to tell a lousy joke that you've heard eight times before.

_____ should be arrested.

_____ always has something wrapped up in a blanket in the back seat of his car.

NAME MALES

_____ goes to the beach but doesn't swim. The only time he gets wet is when the girl he's with brings back a bathing-cap-full of water and pours it on his stomach. Then he wrestles with her and gets sand in the food.

_____ never volunteers to get anything or help out; but he makes wise cracks when some good-natured fellow does volunteer.

_____ calls up disc jockeys with requests.

_____ wears a blue suit with brown shoes.

_____ is always talking to someone else's wife.

_____ is a pessimist. He makes out his will when he's twenty-five.

_____ is the only fellow who can find a way to get a drink at a P.T.A. meeting.

WHAT NOT TO
NAME   FEMALES

_____ lies about her age before anybody asks her.

_____ can never go out because she just this minute finished washing her hair.

_____ thinks she's a living doll but she's never gotten a good look at herself from the rear.

_____ is always saying "I'm not interested in playing around. I am interested in getting married, nothing else." But she will go out with anyone who calls at six-thirty.

_____ should buy a new girdle.

_____ should buy a new girdle and an uplift bra.

_____ should buy a new girdle, an uplift bra, and have her hair washed.

NAME　　　　　FEMALES

_____ always orders anything on the menu that she can't pronounce.

_____ shaves her legs, but not often enough.

_____ is nearsighted and won't wear her glasses and people think she is snooty.

_____ never lets you forget that she graduated from college. She never lets her husband forget either.

_____ goes on crying jags if you don't watch her.

_____ acts like she's the only woman in the world who ever had a baby.

_____ gets to a party, and before she meets anyone she runs into the washroom and combs her hair for ten minutes.

NAME   FEMALES

_____ telephones at 2 A.M. and says, "Guess who this is."

_____ likes to have her portrait drawn in store windows.

POSTSCRIPT

I FEEL CERTAIN *that this small volume will one day take its place with comparable works which have influenced the direction of man's thought—works such as Goethe's* Die Natur, *Darwin's* Origin of the Species *and Stern's* Son of Mad Libs.

I can see the time coming when all personality problems may be solved by professional name changers who may be called Name Analysts. If GEORGE is tired of being imposed on and feels he's a failure, he goes to a Name Analyst who gives him a new first name (changing the last name is of no significance). The new name is CLARK. No one is going to impose on CLARK. CLARK marries a wealthy girl (DEEDY?) and becomes an executive in her father's company.

Or perhaps GEORGE gets the name DINO. He becomes an Italian, takes voice lessons, and gets his own TV show.

So, if you're a prospective parent and have your child's best interests at heart, think carefully before naming it. Remember, you can't escape by giving it an odd name. You name a boy ULYSSES, TECUMSEH, LUCIUS or OMAR and chances are he'll become a General. Girls named TALLULAH or ZSA ZSA always grow up to be TALLULAH or ZSA ZSA.

Whatever you do when choosing a name, stay away from ADOLPH, GAMALIAL and MAO. We have enough trouble in the world as is.

MIDGE always hates to say goodbye.

This is a **PRICE/STERN/SLOAN** *Publishers, Inc.* book.

Other splendid P/S/S books are:

You Were Born On A Rotten Day
First Wife, Second Wife
It's Over When . . .
How To Be An Italian
How To Be A Jewish Mother
Shelley Berman's Cleans & Dirtys
What Ever Happened To . . . ?
The Mad Libs series
The VIP Notebook
and many, many more

They are available at your bookseller's, or may be ordered directly from the publisher. For free brochure write:

Dept. W-12

PRICE/STERN/SLOAN *Publishers, Inc.*

410 N. La Cienega Boulevard
Los Angeles, California 90048